## Viewpoints and Perspectives

# THE SINKING OF THE TITANIC

★ PART OF THE PERSPECTIVES LIBRARY ★

KRISTIN J. RUSSO

Published in the United States of America by Cherry Lake Publishing
Ann Arbor, Michigan
www.cherrylakepublishing.com

Reading Adviser: Marla Conn MS, Ed., Literacy specialist, Read-Ability, Inc.

Photo Credits: ©Lisa-Blue/Getty Images, 1 (left); ©Wikimedia, 1 (middle); ©Wikimedia, 1 (right); ©Lisa-Blue/Getty Images, cover (left); ©Wikimedia, cover (middle); ©Wikimedia, cover (right); ©Lisa-Blue/Getty Images, 4; ©English Heritage/Newscom,7; ©Richard Graulich/The Palm Beach Post/ZUMAPRESS/Newscom,9; ©Everett Historical/Shutterstock, 10; ©Wikimedia, 13; ©Wikimedia, 14; ©Wikimedia, 16; ©Wikimedia, 18; ©Wikimedia, 19; ©Wikimedia, 20; ©Wikimedia, 22; ©The Print Collector / Heritage-Images/Newscom,26; ©akg-images/Newscom,27; ©Wikipedia Commons Public Domain/ZUMAPRESS/Newscom,31; ©Wikimedia, 32; ©Tommy Lindholm/Pacific Press/Newscom,35; ©Ralph White/Wikimedia, 36; ©UPPA/Photoshot/Newscom,38; ©World History Archive/Newscom,43; ©Wikimedia, 44; ©antoniradso/Shutterstock, 45

Copyright ©2019 by Cherry Lake Publishing
All rights reserved. No part of this book may be reproduced or utilized in
any form or by any means without written permission from the publisher.

Library of Congress Cataloging-in-Publication Data has been filed and is available at catalog.loc.gov

Cherry Lake Publishing would like to acknowledge the work of The Partnership for 21st Century Learning.
Please visit *www.p21.org* for more information.

Printed in the United States of America
Corporate Graphics

# Table of Contents

In this book, you will read about the RMS *Titanic*'s sinking from three perspectives. Each perspective is based on real things that happened to real people who were aboard the ship. As you'll see, the same event can look different depending on one's point of view.

**Chapter 1** .................................................................... 4
Mrs. Rhoda Abbott: Third Class Passenger

**Chapter 2** ................................................................... 18
Eva Hart: Second Class Passenger

**Chapter 3** ................................................................... 32
Mr. Jacob Astor: Property and Real Estate Developer,
First Class Passenger

**Timeline** ................................................................... 44

**Look, Look Again** ................................................ 46

**Glossary** ................................................................... 47

**Learn More** ............................................................ 47

**Index** ......................................................................... 48

**About the Author** ................................................ 48

# 1

# Mrs. Rhoda Abbott

## Third Class Passenger

**I** was born and raised in England, you see. I did not move to the United States until I was a young woman. I married a man from London, and we started our life in Providence, Rhode Island, but it never felt like home. When my life grew difficult, I grew homesick and decided to sail home and live with my widowed mother. I needed comfort and security. I tell you all this so that you will know. I understand homesickness, truly I do. And that is why I made the most terrible decision of my life.

> **THINK ABOUT IT**
> Determine the main point of the first paragraph and pick out one piece of evidence that supports it.

My marriage ended in 1911. Stanton was a good man in the beginning. Oh, and what charisma he had. He was a champion too! He was the United States middleweight boxing champion. What strength, what energy he had! Our boys, Rossmore and Eugene, were the joys of our life together. But we couldn't make it work. In the end, we both decided to separate. It's hard for a woman to make it on her own, and I had my boys to consider. Oh! And I was so homesick. My father had died, and my mother needed company. It made the most sense for everyone for me to return home to England.

At first, it seemed as though we would thrive. I became a seamstress, and Rossmore learned boot making and even considered becoming a jeweler. Eugene was still a schoolboy and had not decided on a career quite yet. But now my boys were homesick. They missed their lives in the United States. They missed their family and friends. I understood their homesickness, and I hated to see them suffer. I decided to sail back to the United States.

On April 10, 1912, the three of us boarded the *Titanic* in Southampton, England. Money was tight, and I had to purchase three tickets, so we took third class accommodations. Originally, we purchased passage on the SS *Philadelphia*. Due to a coal strike, the *Philadelphia* did not sail, and we were happy to be offered berths on the *Titanic*, even if they were third class accommodations.

Third class is also called steerage class. Passengers' cabins are so low in the ship, they are near the cables that move the steering rudders. I felt like steerage leaving my home. I felt very low. But my

THE RMS *OLYMPIC*, BUILT ALONGSIDE THE *TITANIC*, HAD A SIMILAR DESIGN USING WATERTIGHT DOORS AND HATCHES THAT WAS MEANT TO MAKE IT "UNSINKABLE."

boys were as happy as I had ever seen them, and I felt I was doing the right thing. Oh! How wrong I was!

**SOS**

The *Titanic* struck the iceberg at 11:40 p.m. on April 14. At 12:15 a.m. on April 15, Captain Smith ordered one of the ship's officers to calculate the exact position of the ship. Then he had the ship's radio operator tap out the first distress signal in Morse code. By the time the ship sank, 70 messages were sent back and forth between the *Titanic* and other ships in the area. Ships of several nationalities started to come to the aid of the *Titanic*. But the ship that was the closest to the *Titanic*, the SS *Californian*, did not receive the distress messages. Its radio operator was asleep.

ONLY 24 PERCENT OF THIRD CLASS PASSENGERS SURVIVED THE SINKING. SECOND CLASS PASSENGERS HAD A 42 PERCENT SURVIVAL RATE, AND 61 PERCENT OF FIRST CLASS PASSENGERS SURVIVED.

A LUNCHEON MENU FROM THE *TITANIC*, DATED APRIL 14, 1912, SHOWS THAT THE DAY THE SHIP SANK, FIRST CLASS PASSENGERS WERE SERVED SOUSED HERRING AND GRILLED MUTTON CHOPS FOR LUNCH.

We were not made to feel like steerage on the voyage—that came later. There was plenty to do on board. We talked and laughed and ate with the other passengers. There was a general room that also served as a nursery, and most would gather there to chat and pass the time playing games or gossiping. Many had brought along musical instruments, and there was dancing and singing. One passenger played his bagpipes to everyone's delight.

Certainly there were areas of the ship where we were not welcome. The first class and second class areas were strictly off limits. But we did have a deck available to us for playing and taking in fresh air. And the food was adequate. There was oatmeal porridge with milk and ham and eggs for breakfast. And the boys devoured the roast beef and gravy with fresh bread at dinner. Tea came with cold meats and cheese. The boys looked happy and healthy. Their happiness lifted my heavy heart.

> **SECOND SOURCE**
>
> Find another source that describes the moment when the iceberg was first seen. Compare the information there to the information in this source.

It was on the fourth night that my hell on earth began. Shortly before midnight—at 11:40 p.m. to be exact—the *Titanic* struck ice. Down in the lower cabins, we felt and heard the ship's impact with the iceberg immediately, but we did not know what exactly had happened. I did not want to overreact and cause the boys angst, so I told them to wait. They were eager to investigate, of course, but my instincts were to wait for instructions. Oh! How I curse those instincts. They set us terribly off course.

I stopped a steward outside our room, and he told us that there was nothing to worry about. That we should return to our beds. And so we did. Only a few minutes later, about 15 minutes after midnight on the next day—April 15—another steward made his way down the hall calling for all to put on life jackets and

THE ICEBERG THAT SANK THE *TITANIC* WAS SPOTTED AT 11:39 P.M. THERE WAS NO TIME FOR THE SHIP TO CHANGE COURSE, AND IT COLLIDED WITH THE ICEBERG ONLY 30 SECONDS LATER.

to move up to the deck.

By the time we opened our door to make our way up, the passageway was filled with people, and we struggled to make our way to the upper deck. After

THE *TITANIC* HAD ENOUGH ROOM TO CARRY 64 LIFEBOATS, BUT ENDED UP CARRYING ONLY 20.

what seemed an eternity, the boys and I made it to the top deck. There were very few lifeboats left, and officers would allow only women with small children in them. At ages 16 and 13, I knew my strapping, healthy boys would not be allowed. I took their hands and stepped away from the lifeboat. I would be allowed in the boat, but I would not leave without them. It was 2:05 a.m. when the last lifeboat was lowered from the ship. I found out later that there were still 1,500 passengers on board. Can you imagine? More than 2,200 passengers were originally on the ship, yet there were lifeboats for only half that many. No wonder so many souls were lost that night. At 2:17 a.m., we received the last communication from the ship's captain, "Every man for himself!"

Suddenly, the ship snapped in half, and the deck on which we were standing went from horizontal to vertical. Rossmore, Eugene, and I were thrown off balance. Holding hands, we all three together were swept into the freezing ocean water.

Frantically, I kicked and splashed and did all I could do to stay afloat. I had to find my sons. Victims screamed for help, yet I had only one mission—to find Rossmore and Eugene. I hollered their names as

Survivors were rescued by the RMS *Carpathia*. *Titanic* passenger Mr. Charles Dahl later reported that the *Carpathia* had to zigzag around several icebergs in "an ice field" to reach *Titanic* survivors.

loudly as I could. Treading water, I knew I would not last long. I knew they would not last long either, unless I found them and we made our way to a lifeboat. Suddenly, I felt an arm grab mine. I was pulled up and over into Lifeboat A. After that moment, all went dark for me. I remained unconscious until I was aboard the *Carpathia*. Neither Rossmore nor Eugene survived.

Later, I received a notice that Rossmore had been found and was buried at sea on April 24, 1912. My darling little Eugene was never found.

# Eva Hart

## Second Class Passenger

Mother says we should not be on this ship. She has had a **premonition** that our journey will not end well. Father is delighted. We were meant to take another ship, the *Philadelphia*, to North America. But when that ship did not sail, we were offered berths on the RMS *Titanic*. Father says the *Titanic* is the ship everyone is talking about. "It is unsinkable," he says. Everyone is saying it! He is thrilled that we are on its maiden voyage. We are traveling to Winnipeg, Manitoba, in Canada. Father wants to go into business for himself. He plans to open a drug store.

EVA HART SURVIVED THE SINKING. ON APRIL 15, 1995, AT THE AGE OF 90, SHE ATTENDED THE OPENING OF A MEMORIAL GARDEN TO HONOR VICTIMS OF THE *TITANIC* AT THE NATIONAL MARITIME MUSEUM IN LONDON, ENGLAND.

THE *TITANIC* WAS BUILT AT THE HARLAND AND WOLFF SHIPYARD ON QUEEN'S ISLAND IN BELFAST, IRELAND. CONSTRUCTION BEGAN ON MARCH 31, 1909.

Mother feels strongly that we should wait and take a different ship. She thinks that to say that something is "unsinkable" is "flying in the face of God." She is not a **superstitious** person by nature and has never had a strong premonition like this. For this reason, I believe her. I agree that something terrible may happen. But what can I do? Father says we shall sail on the *Titanic*, and that is what we will do.

As we boarded on April 10, 1912, at Southampton, England, Mother planted her feet and refused to budge. Her premonition was so strong, she could not make herself move forward up the **gangplank**. But Father persuaded her that all would be well. After all, we are due to dock in New York in only one week, on April 17. What could go wrong in only one week? It is not like the old days when ships were months at sea. The *Titanic* is strong and fast. Father has persuaded her. Soon, she followed him, with me by the hand.

She told him she would not sleep on the ship, and so far, she hasn't. Each night she sits up in a chair, fully dressed, ready to face whatever catastrophe she believes will befall us. This makes me uncomfortable,

A HEATED SWIMMING POOL WAS AVAILABLE TO FIRST CLASS PASSENGERS ABOARD THE *TITANIC*.

I admit. I have trouble falling asleep knowing that Mother is awake. She reads and sews. Father sleeps soundly.

At breakfast, Father teases me. He asks if I would like some grilled ox kidneys. "It's on the menu!" he says, and shows me. I make a face. He has found the only thing on the menu I do not think that I would like. Today I will have grilled ham and fried eggs. Tomorrow I might have the buckwheat cakes with maple syrup. The food on board is yummy, and I am never hungry. For dinner, we have chicken, lamb, or turkey, and boiled or roasted potatoes. And for dessert—my favorite!—we have plum pudding or American ice cream.

I spend most of the days outside on deck, playing with my new friend, Nana Harper. We play ring toss or shuffleboard with the other children. We also have a library, and we children are allowed to choose our own books. I do not read very much. I am too excited! And Mother is too anxious to sit with me and read. She is becoming more and more nervous as our journey at sea goes on.

It is our fourth day of travel. We are more than half way there! I spend the day as I normally do,

> **ANALYZE THIS**
> Analyze two accounts in this book that describe the moment when passengers first learned the ship was in trouble and they needed to leave their rooms. How are they different?

playing outdoors and eating the delicious food. Father reads to me when Mother cannot. Her nervousness is particularly strong today. I wish she could relax and enjoy herself aboard this magnificent ship, especially now that our journey is almost over.

Father and I go to bed early, so tired are we from playing outdoors and walking along the deck and **promenade**. Mother sits in her chair, again, fully dressed and ready for disaster. This makes me toss and turn. When Mother cannot relax, I cannot relax. Father begins to snore.

Just before midnight, Mother and I feel movement. It is like a small jerk, like when a train comes to a stop at the station. Immediately Mother is on her feet. She wakes Father and sends him to the deck to find out what has happened. At first he resists.

He has not felt anything strange. How could he? He was sound asleep. But Mother insists and Father finally agrees.

In the meantime, Mother gets me up out of bed and begins to dress me. I resist this too. I am comfortable in my warm bed. Surely, Mother is overreacting. She wrestles me into my dress and stockings and shoes. She is just buttoning up my warm coat when Father arrives back at the cabin.

My parents say nothing to one another. My mother does not even ask what has happened. It is as if she knows, and she does not need my father to explain. The catastrophe she has been waiting for has arrived. My father wraps a warm blanket around me as if I were a little baby. Then he wraps my mother in his warmest coat. He puts on a coat as well, and we all move silently to the lift—the elevator—that will take us to the top deck. Father carries me the whole way.

When we arrived on deck, Father placed me in

Lifeboat 14. He helped my mother in as well. "Hold Mummy's hand and be a good girl," he told me. Then, he disappeared. The lifeboats were for women and

THERE WERE ABOUT 3,500 LIFE JACKETS ON BOARD THE SHIP. HOWEVER, THEY DID NOT KEEP VICTIMS FROM FREEZING TO DEATH IN THE COLD WATER.

Seventy-five percent of female passengers survived. Only 20 percent of male passengers survived. Two lap dogs also survived—they were brought aboard lifeboats by their owners.

children, and he could not join us.

It was after Father left us that I felt panic truly rise up in my throat. Mother and I were alone! How would we go on without him? It took quite a while, but finally our lifeboat was lowered into the ocean. The ice-cold wind **penetrated** my coat and blanket, and I shivered next to Mother, who tried her best to keep me warm. Though no one ever explained to me what

## THE COST OF A TICKET

How much did it cost to travel on the *Titanic*? Only the very rich could afford first class cabins. A ticket for a cabin cost $150 (about $3,500 today). For a first class parlor suite with three or four rooms, the price was more than $4,000 (about $100,000 today). A ticket in steerage cost between $15 and $40 (about $350 to $930 today).

was happening, I could see quite clearly that the *Titanic* was sinking!

Our boat was overfull, but we rowed and rowed as fast as we could from the sinking ship. Mother explained that if we were too close to the ship when it went under, we would be pulled under as well. The suction in the ocean would pull our lifeboat back and under. So we rowed and rowed.

> **THINK ABOUT IT**
> What is the main idea of this chapter? Give three reasons why you think this.

Our boat wasn't the only lifeboat that had too many people in it, yet there were some lifeboats that were barely filled at all. A ship's mate reassigned us to different boats to make it all more even. This was safer for all, but I was separated from Mother in the process. Now, I was truly terrified!

I had nothing to do but sit quietly and watch the **chaos** unfold before me. I saw the lights on the *Titanic* dim and then go out completely. I saw the ship split in half and then sink entirely. I heard the screams of the passengers who did not make it onto lifeboats. Then, I heard the terrible silence when the screaming stopped. Soon, there was nothing left of the ship.

After what seemed like hours, another ship appeared on the horizon. It was called the *Carpathia*. The grown-up passengers climbed a rope ladder to safety, but we children could not climb. Instead, we were wrapped in mail sacks and pulled up in a net by a pulley. I was terrified that I would slip through the net and into the ocean!

Finally, I was pulled safely aboard the *Carpathia* and reunited with my mother. My father **perished** that terrible night. I never saw him again.

The first lifeboat was launched with only 28 people in it, even though it had room for 65. Ultimately, 472 seats aboard lifeboats went unfilled.

# 3

# Mr. Jacob Astor
## Property and Real Estate Developer, First Class Passenger

I can put it off no longer. It is time to go home. But at least we can go home in style.

One cannot blame me for needing to escape. Before we left, New York society could talk of nothing but my divorce from Ava and my marriage to Madeleine. Madeleine is beautiful, but it is true that she is very young, only 18. It was obvious right after our wedding that I had to take my new bride away. Our marriage was **scandalous** to some, and Madeleine suffered from mean stares and cold remarks from my so-called "friends." We decided a winter vacation in Egypt and Paris would be just the thing. But now that Madeleine is expecting our first child, it is time we return home to New York.

    Few know this, but I am a bit of a tinkerer. I love to know how things work. I love the mechanics of engines and how all the cogs and wheels work together to make a thing go. Naturally, I do not like to brag, but I am particularly proud of my inventions—particularly a new and improved bicycle brake. My "tinkering" has even helped to create what is called an improved **turbine** engine. I am beyond delighted to be traveling on the *Titanic*, the unsinkable *Titanic*. I hope very much that I will be able to spend time with the ship's designer, Thomas Andrews. He will have a wealth of knowledge about mechanics and engineering. The time will pass most pleasantly, I believe, if I can spend much of it with Mr. Andrews.

Indeed, I will be joined by many friends and acquaintances on our voyage home. Mr. Benjamin Guggenheim and Mr. and Mrs. Isidor and Rosalie Ida Straus are on board, as are Sir Cosmo and Lady Duff-Gordon. Lady Duff-Gordon is a top fashion designer. I am certain Madeleine will enjoy her company. There is also the rather loud and **uncouth** Mrs. Margaret Brown. She insists upon being called Molly. I hope to avoid her company, but of course I would never be impolite.

Captain Edward John Smith says the *Titanic* is making excellent time, and we should arrive at White Star Line's pier 60 in New York on Wednesday, April 17, on schedule. This is despite the delays getting started. There was a coal strike in Europe, you see, and many ships could not be outfitted with enough coal to sail. In fact, the *Titanic* was supplied with coal from

THERE WERE 39 PRIVATE FIRST CLASS SUITES ABOARD THEY *TITANIC*. THEY FEATURED EXPENSIVE DECOR IN GEORGIAN AND QUEEN ANNE STYLES.

other ships, which naturally cancelled their planned voyages.

Captain Smith tells me that another near-accident added to the *Titanic*'s difficult start. As it was pulled out into the River Test by tugboats, the *Titanic* nearly collided with the USMS *New York*. The **undertow** caused by the *Titanic* caused the *New York* to snap her moorings, and she missed colliding with the *Titanic* by

Captain Edward J. Smith, right, was the highest-paid ship's captain at the end of the 19th century. He took command of the *Titanic* on April 1, 1912, and went down with the ship on April 15.

only 4 feet (1.2 meters). See? What luck! The *Titanic* truly is unsinkable!

Though the ship is moving quickly, it is a joy to spend these last few days with Madeleine before we rejoin New York society. She and I walk the promenade, making sure we take the time to stop and rest. She tires easily these days. Her appetite is healthy, which is good since there are certainly **culinary** delights beyond measure at the dinner table. Just today at luncheon, we both had our fill of roast beef, grilled mutton chops, veal and ham pie, and delectable desserts such as custard pudding and apple meringue.

Then, for me at least, it is off to the gymnasium to exercise away luncheon before dinner. Perhaps I'll find an opponent for a **squash** match or work with the

> **SECOND SOURCE**
>
> Find another source that describes what it was like to be a first class passenger. Compare that information to this source.

**AMENITIES FOUND ON THE FIRST CLASS DECK INCLUDED A GYMNASIUM, A PARISIAN CAFÉ, A LIBRARY, A KENNEL FOR PASSENGERS' PETS, AND A SMOKING ROOM.**

personal trainer on board through a series of stationary bicycling, rowing, and even weight training. Ironically, there is a swimming pool on board. It is 6 feet (1.8 m) deep and filled with heated salt water. A much more pleasant swim, I daresay, than a dip in the Atlantic Ocean!

I am most entertained in the evenings. Madeleine retires early and does not join me in the first class smoking room—which is for men only. But it is no matter that I do not have my dear wife with me. I find the most accomplished and most interesting characters to speak with. I have discussed engineering and design with Thomas Andrews, just as I had hoped. I have also had the pleasure of discussing politics with Major Archibald Butt, an aide to President William Howard Taft. And muralist Frank Millet expounds on his knowledge of art and painting. There is so much to learn! And there is a bit of sport, I will admit. Each day we bet on the speed that the ship will make in a day. This is no real gambling den, just a bit of fun to pass the time.

Oh! What a bother! We are four days in to our journey and it is nearly midnight, yet there is some commotion up on deck. It is highly unusual. Perhaps I should go investigate, if nothing else than to put Madeleine's mind at ease. It appears we have hit an

## WHO'S WHO

The *Titanic* was the most fashionable way for wealthy people to travel by ship. Because of that, many famous passengers were aboard. Isidor Straus, who started the Macy's department store, died with his wife, Rosalie Ida. Benjamin Guggenheim was another wealthy man on board. As the ship sank, he is remembered as saying, "We've dressed in our best and are prepared to go down like gentlemen." Probably the most famous *Titanic* survivor was Margaret Tobin Brown. She was a wealthy and brave woman who tried to get Lifeboat 6 to return to the site of the sinking to find survivors. She was given the nickname "the unsinkable Molly Brown."

iceberg. I cannot imagine this will be too serious an issue. The *Titanic* is unsinkable, after all.

Rather than join the throngs of panicked passengers on deck, I escort Madeleine to the gymnasium. Here we sit in relative comfort atop the mechanical horses. They are not meant for leisure—they are meant for vigorous exercise! But I feel this is the safest place for us. It's certainly wiser to stay aboard the ship than to drop into the ocean in one of those tiny lifeboats!

Madeleine is getting agitated. I have procured lifebelts for us both, but she is not certain it will keep her afloat. I find another, and with my pocket knife, I rip it open to show her that, indeed, the lifebelt is filled with material that floats.

Madeleine's agitation increases. I will go to check once more on the best course of action. I stop a second officer and ask what we should do. He appears shocked that we haven't already made our way to the lifeboats.

As it is, we will have to climb through the windows of the enclosed promenade to get to the deck. All other passageways are now blocked by people clamoring to make it to the deck to climb aboard a lifeboat. With my help, Madeleine makes it through an open window.

When I attempt to join her, an officer, Charles Lightoller is his name, stops me. Only women and children are allowed, he tells me.

Madeleine resists leaving me, and I ask if I might join her, considering her pregnancy. Lightoller tells me that only women and children are allowed in the lifeboats, and that no man can enter until all the women have been safely secured. I must calm Madeleine down and compel her to do the right thing for herself and the baby. "The ladies have to go first. Get in the lifeboat, to please me. Good-bye, dearie. I'll see you later," I tell her.

### ANALYZE THIS

Analyze two narratives in this book that describe the moment when the passengers were getting into lifeboats. How are they different?

I ask Lightoller in which lifeboat I will find her. He tells me boat number 4. Boat number 4. If it is at all possible for me to find her again, I will ask after the passengers in Lifeboat 4. I watch as her boat is lowered into the sea. Others panic, trying to free the remaining lifeboats. I stand alone and watch. The cold wind chills me to my bones. The water will be even colder. I do not believe that I will live to learn the fate of Lifeboat 4.

ASTOR'S FUNERAL TOOK PLACE ON MAY 4, 1912.

# TIMELINE
## THE *TITANIC*

The *Titanic* leaves Southampton, England, to begin its voyage across the Atlantic Ocean.

**APRIL 10, 1912**

At 1:45 p.m., a nearby ship, the *Amerika*, reports two large icebergs. The *Titanic* does not receive this message directly, but was supposed to receive it when it came in range of the *Amerika*'s transmitter. Iceberg warnings continue throughout the day.

**APRIL 14, 1912**

A warning from the Baltic about the two icebergs finally reaches the bridge on the *Titanic*. A second officer orders crew in the crow's nest to "keep a sharp lookout for ice."

**7:15 P.M. APRIL 14, 1912**

**11:39 P.M. APRIL 14, 1912**

Frederick Fleet calls the bridge directly from the crow's nest. "Iceberg right ahead!" he reports. The *Titanic* turns to the left.

**11:40 P.M. APRIL 14, 1912**

The *Titanic* strikes an iceberg. The crew closes watertight doors as the ship begins to flood. Captain Smith returns to the bridge.

**12:00 MIDNIGHT APRIL 15, 1912**

Thomas Andrews reports to Captain Smith that the ship will stay afloat for only about two hours.

**2:20 A.M. APRIL 15, 1912**

The *Titanic* is completely submerged.

# Look, Look Again

Take a close look at this illustration of the sinking of the *Titanic* and answer the following questions:

1. How would a mother who had lost sight of her children describe this scene? What would the woman, who had been pulled from the water into the safety of a lifeboat, think when looking at this scene?

2. What would a little girl who was separated from both of her parents see in this picture? What would she think of the other passengers that she could see were in the water? What would she want to do? Why?

3. What would a man who was used to a life of luxury think about this scene, knowing he would not be allowed on a lifeboat? How would he feel to be separated from his family?

# GLOSSARY

**chaos** *(KAY-oss)* disorder and confusion

**culinary** *(KUHL-uh-ner-ee)* having to do with cooking

**gangplank** *(GANG-plangk)* a moveable ramp people use to board or leave a ship

**penetrate** *(PEN-ih-treyt)* to force a way through

**perish** *(PEHR-ish)* to suffer death in a sudden or untimely way

**premonition** *(prem-uh-NISH-uhn)* a strong feeling that something unpleasant is going to happen

**promenade** *(prom-uh-NAHD)* a place created for public walking

**scandalous** *(SKAN-dl-us)* dishonorable or improper

**squash** *(SKWASH)* a game in which two players use rackets to hit a small, soft rubber ball against the walls of a closed court

**superstitious** *(soo-per-STISH-uhs)* believing in things that are irrational or cannot be proven

**turbine** *(TUR-bahyn)* a machine that produces continuous power

**uncouth** *(uhn-KOOTH)* lacking sophistication or good manners

**undertow** *(UHN-der-toh)* a strong current that causes a hazard to swimmers

# LEARN MORE

## FURTHER READING

Price, Sean. *Passengers of the Titanic: Traveling on an Ill-Fated Ship*. North Mankato, MN: Capstone Press, 2015.

Sabol, Stephanie. *What Was the Titanic?* New York: Penguin Workshop, 2018.

Zullo, Allan. *Titanic Young Survivors*. New York: Scholastic, 2012.

## WEBSITES

**Stories of Survivors**
https://www.biography.com/news/titanics-100th-anniversary-6-survivor-stories-20799733
This website explains more about what happened to survivors after the tragic sinking.

**The *Titanic***
https://www.britannica.com/topic/Titanic
This website describes the construction, sailing, and sinking of the RMS *Titanic*.

# INDEX

Andrews, Thomas, 33, 34, 39, 45

Brown, Margaret Tobin, 40

*Carpathia*, 16, 17, 30

England, 4, 5, 6, 19, 21, 44

icebergs, 8, 12, 13, 41, 45

lifeboats, 14, 15, 17, 25, 26, 27, 28, 29, 31, 40, 41, 42, 43, 46

life jackets, 12, 26

Morse code, 8

New York, 21, 32, 33, 34, 36, 37

*Olympic*, 7

*Philadelphia*, 6, 18

Smith, Captain Edward John, 8, 15, 34, 35, 36, 45

SOS, 8

tickets, 6, 28

# ABOUT THE AUTHOR

Kristin J. Russo is a university English lecturer. She loves teaching, reading, writing, and learning new things. She and her husband live near Providence, Rhode Island, in a small house surrounded by flower gardens. They have three grown children and three rescue dogs.